THE GIFT of KNOWING
Our Heavenly Father

Abiding in Intimacy

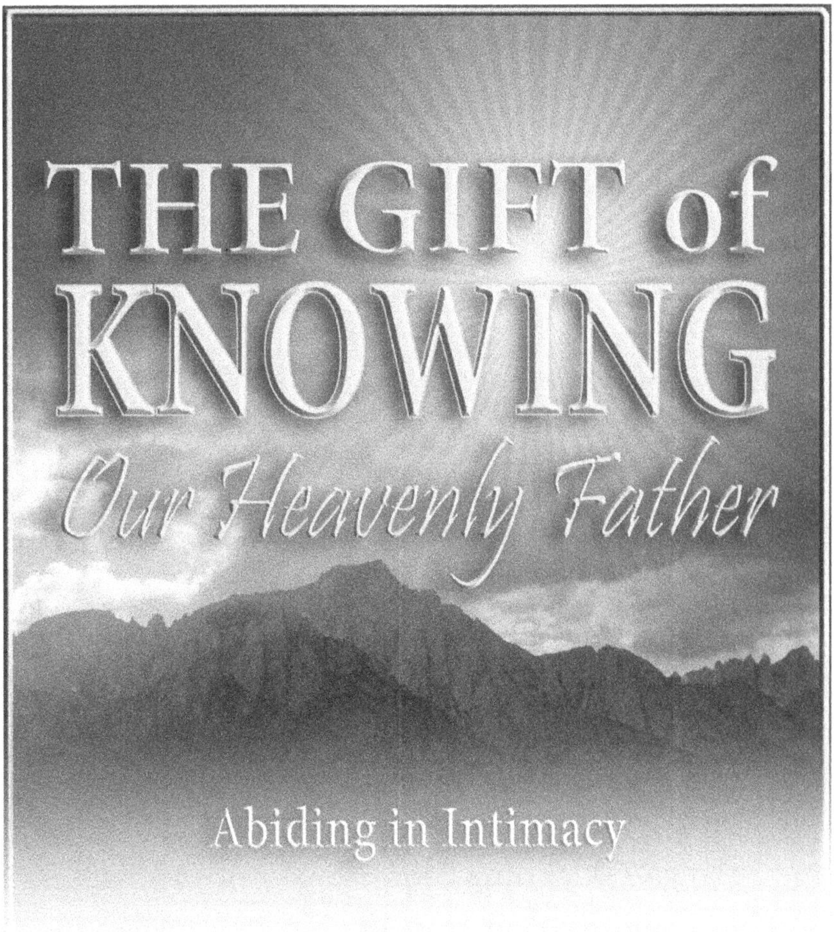

THE GIFT of KNOWING Our Heavenly Father

Abiding in Intimacy

by
Deborah K. Reed

Christian Literature & Artwork
A BOLD TRUTH Publication

THE GIFT of KNOWING Our Heavenly Father
Copyright © 2015 Deborah K. Reed

ISBN 13: 978-0-9965908-1-5

BOLD TRUTH PUBLISHING
Christian Literature & Artwork
300 West 41st
Sand Springs, Oklahoma 74067
www.BoldTruthPublishing.com
beirep@yahoo.com

Printed in the USA.

All rights reserved under International Copyright Law. All contents and/or cover art and design may not be reproduced in whole or in part in any form without the express written consent of the Author.

The views expressed in this book are not necessarily those of the publisher.

We would like to recognize and thank these Publiishers, for publishing and distributing the following versions of God's written Word.

The Lord gave the word: great was the company of those that published it. - Psalm 68:11 (KJV)

"Scripture quotations marked (AMP) are taken from the Amplified® Bible, Copyright © 1954, 1958, 1962, 1964, 1965, 1987 by The Lockman Foundation Used by permission." (www.Lockman.org)

Scriptures marked KJV are taken from the KING JAMES VERSION (KJV): KING JAMES VERSION, public domain.

"Scripture marked THE MESSAGE are taken from The Message Bible. Copyright © 1993, 1994, 1995, 1996, 2000, 2001, 2002. Used by permission of NavPress Publishing Group."

Scripture quotations marked (NLT) are taken from the Holy Bible, New Living Translation, Copyright © 1996, 2004, 2007 by Tyndale House Foundation. Used by permission of Tyndale House Publishers, Inc., Carol Stream, IL 60188. All rights reserved.

Contents

Dedication..*i*
Author's Preface...*ii*
Introduction 1

Chapter 1
Life in Christ...3
God is True Love..8
Intimacy with God..9
Breakthrough...10
Secret Place...11

Chapter 2
Resting in Him..13
None Greater...18

Chapter 3
Covenant Relationship..19
Love..23
God's Presence..24
Jerusalem, Jerusalem..25
Midnight Hour..26

Chapter 4
Our Inheritance..27
A Psalm...31
Here I Am..32
Love of Jesus...33
Jesus...34
Oh Daddy God...35

Survival of the Fetus	36
All About Him	37
Alone	38
Forgiveness	39
Yesterday is Gone	40
Eyes on Jesus	41
Faith	42
Holy Ghost	43
Favor	44
Best Friend	45
Children	46
Prosperity	47
Birthday	48
Behind	49
Healed	50
A Mother's Cry	51
Arise, Oh Church	52
Resting	53
One God	54
Awakening	55
Prophecy	56
Prophecies	58
Conclusion	60
A Soul Winner's Heart	62
Prayer for Salvation	63
Reference Scriptures	65

Dedication

I dedicate this book to
my heavenly Father and Jesus my Lord.
They get all the glory.
I give thanks to my family and friends
who encouraged me with these gifts.
Amen

Author's Preface

How to Enter the Holy of Holies

Written by Deborah K. Reed
2000

1. Outer Court
*Everyone that asketh receiveth.
We ask, make our requests known,
and receive His blessings.
(Read Matthew 7:7)*

2. Inner Court
*This is where we seek Him and have intercession,
waiting until He finds us
(Read Jeremiah 29:11 and Isaiah 40:31)*

3. Holy of Holies
*He draws us in, with quietness.
It is here that we have intimate communion with God.
His presence overwhlems us.*

Introduction

There are many things in life to know about. Knowing is something that never changes, it's forever. *Know* – def. – Understand, a firm grasp of. *Knowing* – def. – Possession of secret inside information of a higher being. I am going to be using this word A LOT in this short book, but remember it as a powerful word. It is useful in each sentence, so you can KNOW the KNOWING.

Knowing we were born of a mother and were given a name and a birthdate. Along with brothers, sisters, and relatives. Knowing that we live in a certain state, on a certain street. Many of us know about our creator; God of Heaven and Earth, people from all nations, animals, flowers, stars, the galaxy, the seas, and all other things. But there is the gift of knowing Him personally and intimately that we can all have. He is there all of the time to listen and hear and love us and help us. But, we must learn how knowing is the biggest part of it all - that you would never doubt for any reason. You must have it in your inner man, the spiritual heart, your REAL being.

God is a spirit and we contact Him in spirit and in truth. I love knowing God and Jesus for They are the ultimate way of life. They are life eternal; forever.

Isaiah 45:8 AMP

Let fall in showers, you heavens, from above, and let the skies rain down righteousness [the pure, spiritual, heaven-born possibilities that have their foundation in the holy being of God]; let the earth open, and let them [skies and earth] sprout forth salvation, and let righteousness germinate and spring up [as plants do] together; I the Lord have created it.

Chapter 1
Life in Christ

Salvation

Knowing we all have a spirit and must be born again, and receiving Him as our Lord and Savior. Knowing we are in a new family, and are just passing through Earth on a journey. Knowing God sent His Son Jesus as a man to share His love and Word. Knowing He went to the cross and was crucified, shedding His blood so men could be free from evil and wickedness. Knowing He sends His Holy Spirit to live inside of us. Knowing we are loved by God as much as He loves His own Son Jesus. Knowing He paid a price for our sins, sicknesses, poverty, lack and diseases.

John 3:6-7 AMP
6. What is born of [from] the flesh is flesh [of the physical is physical]; and what is born of the Spirit is spirit.
7. Marvel not [do not be surprised, astonished] at My telling you, You must all be born anew (from above).

Freedom

Knowing we are free from fear, hate, selfishness, greed, and loneliness. Knowing He is our protector, advocate, comforter, counselor, strengthener, and stand-by. He also intercedes for us. Knowing He makes a way, when there seems no way. Knowing you don't have to earn your way to heaven. It is by faith and grace, in Him, to have eternal life. Knowing we can have Heaven on Earth right now.

John 8:36 AMP
So if the Son liberates you [makes you free men], then you are really and unquestionably free.

Guarantee

Knowing He is a supernatural God, Who can do the impossible. Knowing we have a covenant that cannot be broken. We have a sure title deed. Knowing He knows every hair on our head in number. Every single one of us. Knowing He knows what everyone is going to do, before they even think about doing it; their thoughts and actions. Knowing you cannot hide from God.

Restoration

Knowing He restores all that has been lost in our lives. Knowing He rekindles relationships, marriages, and friendships. Knowing He mends broken hearts, fixes memories from wounded events.

Atonement

Knowing every stripe on His back was meant for our healing and salvation. Knowing the thorns in His crown was for us. Knowing the spear in His side was for our hearts and poverty. Knowing the holes in His hands and feet were for cleansing. Knowing He went to hell and disarmed Satan. Knowing He was resurrected. Glory Hallelujah to Jesus, the Lion of Judah!!

> *Isaiah 53:5 NLT*
> *But he was pierced for our rebellion,*
> *crushed for our sins.*
> *He was beaten so we could be whole.*
> *He was whipped so we could be healed.*

Provision

Knowing He led his people out of bondage. Knowing He kept their shoes and clothes from wearing out for 40 years. Knowing He rained down manna from Heaven and fed them every day. Knowing He supplied money, gave money to the poor. Knowing He healed the sick, raised the dead, delivered those crippled and those possessed by Satan. Knowing He opened prison doors and set His people free. Knowing when we received Him He has given us the same authority in His Name to do even greater works than we thought we were capable of. Knowing that He has blessed us and we are a blessing to Him.

Righteousness

Knowing He made us righteous; right standing with Him. Knowing we sit beside Him in Heaven and that we are His heirs. Knowing He has bestowed bountiful gifts in us. Knowing He has given us all things to enjoy. Knowing He doesn't bring sickness and disaster on you. Knowing we are not condemned nor guilty. Knowing we win; for in Him, we never lose.

> *Ephesians 4:24 KJV*
> *And that ye put on the new man, which after God is created in righteousness and true holiness.*

Anointing

Knowing we are His anointed, His beloved. Knowing we have His power to save the lost, heal the sick, raise the dead, and support others. Knowing He has a plan to have us prosper, not to harm us. Knowing He is responsible for the miracles. Knowing we have the anointing to speak in tongues, a beautiful language bestowed upon us. Knowing He gives us knowledge and understanding. Knowing there is no distance in the spiritual realm.

> *1 John 2:27 AMP*
> *But as for you, the anointing (the sacred appointment, the unction) which you received from Him abides [permanently] in you; [so] then you have no need that anyone should instruct you. But just as*

His anointing teaches you concerning everything and is true and is no falsehood, so you must abide in (live in, never depart from) Him [being rooted in Him, knit to Him], just as [His anointing] has taught you [to do].

Heirs

Knowing when you receive Jesus, you received all He is and all He has. Knowing He has equipped us as Kings and Queens for His work and glory. Knowing we became a new creature, joined with Him, one with Him.

Knowing He gives us all spiritual blessings in heavenly places. Knowing we are robed with His righteousness. Knowing He has crowned us with His glory how magnificently we are richly endowed.

Hallelujah!

God is True Love
Written by Deborah K. Reed

Father God is the creator of all things in this world. His greatest gift was Jesus. He gave His only Son for us to reconnect with Him. His desire was to have a family of many sons and daughters. He loves to fellowship with His people. He asks that we desire time with Him and that He will be first in our lives. We have such wonderful blessings because of His grace. God is good and kind. His plans are wonderful for us. Nothing is more rewarding than His love, peace, and joy for us. He is ever giving. He waits every day for us to come in and love, honor, and praise Him in quiet. Allow Him to have all of you. In His presence, we are filled with His life. He transforms us into His image. He is the most rewarding relationship you could ever have. Love so divine, we can abide in His vine. His love is the purest. He looks to and fro, seeing who He can bless from a willing heart towards Him. We can have this great love filling us each day. We can unite together and be victorious in this world. And bring others to salvation. A living faith, enjoying who we are in Christ. We are the light in the darkness. Changed by God's power to blessed living.

Abiding in Intimacy

Intimacy with God

Written by Deborah K. Reed
June 2015

*We can know true intimacy
as we come in quietness of body, soul, and spirit.
God wants to be full in our life.
Spending quality time alone in His presence
assures us how loved we truly are.*

*I am learning that pursuing intimacy with my Lord,
brings me the greatest joy
in reaching my purpose in life
with Him and others.*

*Reading our Bible, meditation and confessing His Word
is learning to know Him.
Also praising and worshipping.
He desires a deeper relationship, He desires intimacy.*

*He wants to infill us with His spirit.
Heart to heart.
Breath to breath.
Such endless love, joy, and peace.*

Breakthrough

Written by Deborah K. Reed
November 3, 1998

I was alone one night, I was fighting a battle.
I knew I best put on my armor
and be strapped to my saddle.
It was dark and gloomy, the wind whistled high.
I kept claiming His promises.
I said I will make it, I will live, not die.
The thunder roared and boomed, lit up the sky.
I put my trust in God, I was soon flying high.
I worshipped, I praised, I came against the fear.
Before you know it, the Holy Spirit came near.
The victory was mine, I knew right then.
For He gave me His authority to overcome sin.
Soon it was light and the stars shown bright.
Everything that was wrong, He made it alright.
Amen

Abiding in Intimacy

Secret Place
Written by Deborah K. Reed

*He who dwells in the secret place of the most high God
shall remain stable under the shadow of the Almighty.
A true worshipper shall worship the Father
in spirit and in truth.
John 4:23*

*God's desire is for each of us
to come daily into a private time to be with Him.
No televisions or cell phones.
This should be our goal each day,
then the rest of our day goes well.
A time in quiet, enjoying our Father,
getting to know Him more and more.*

*Learning to abide in him fills us to bear much fruit.
John 15:5*

*We enter his gates with thanksgiving
and his courts with praise.
Psalms 69:30-31*

We honor and glorify Him for loving us,

*for being our Father
and Jesus being out Lord and Saviour.
Celebrating our salvation,
being part of His family.*

*We enjoy His anointing in us
and liquid love flowing through us.
The peace and joy He gives us.*

*Read Scriptures for the day,
meditate on what you read.
Pray prayers for the day.
Then be still for awhile,
enjoying His utmost presence.*

*Being surrendered to Him,
He transforms us into Christlike character.
Our spiritual eyes and ears are open to see supernaturally.
God looks to and fro seeing
who will come and abide with Him.*

*I am your first love and I am ever present with you always,
keeping you resting in Me.
Our Father desires intimacy. I am yours,*

*I want you to be all mine.
Be still and know that I am God.
Isaiah 46:10*

Chapter 2
Resting in Him

His Word

Knowing we have His authority to speak His Word in faith. Knowing it will come to pass. Knowing you can do all things in Him. Knowing you can hear His Voice inside your spirit to warn, to guide, to reveal future events. Telling you how to pray, how to speak, how to love, and to obey and submit.

> *2 Corinthians 4:13 KJV*
> *We having the same spirit of faith, according as it is written, I believed, and therefore have I spoken; we also believe, and therefore speak;*

His Presence

Knowing you are consumed with His presence each and every day, every minute, every second. Knowing His sweet fragrance and are arms around you. Knowing you can go into His throne of grace, and adore Him with honor. Exalt Him, lift Him up. Knowing you are the richest person in the universe, for you have His love and presence living inside of you. Knowing He will never leave you or forsake you.

Matthew 28:20b NLT
And be sure of this: I am with you always, even to the end of the age."

Favored

Knowing He is ever merciful and kind. Knowing His goodness never ends. Knowing we are His precious children and He is pleased with us. Knowing we are highly favored. Knowing He lavished wisdom and understanding upon us. Knowing He chose us beforehand, gave us an inheritance. Knowing He has given us angels to send out and work for us and protect us from harm.

Omnipresent

Knowing every breath you take, every step you take, He is with us. The Holy Spirit is alive in us. Knowing we are forgiven of all sin and grace is abounding in and on us. Knowing He is merciful and compassionate to us. Knowing God has great plans for His saints. Knowing when we surrender to Him and rest in His finished work, He will perform what He promised. Knowing He is such a wonderful Father and that Jesus is our King. Knowing when we stumble, He will be there to pick us up. Knowing His love is endless and His power is unmatchable. Knowing He is the Alpha and the Omega. Knowing Jesus and the Holy Spirit are the greatest gifts of all time.

Hebrews 4:13 AMP
And not a creature exists that is concealed from His sight, but all things are open and exposed, naked and defenseless to the eyes of Him with Whom we have to do.

Omniscient

Knowing He delights in us when we sing psalms and songs to Him. Knowing you don't have any fear or concern, for He will handle it for you. Knowing He knows your every thought. Knowing He will mold you into the beautiful person He intended you to be. Like a caterpillar in a cocoon before it blooms into a butterfly. Knowing He will show us mysteries, bring our dreams and visions to pass.

Hebrews 4:12 THE MESSAGE
God means what he says. What he says goes. His powerful Word is sharp as a surgeon's scalpel, cutting through everything, whether doubt or defense, laying us open to listen and obey.

Trust

Knowing we can always trust Him. Knowing He has conquered fear and doubt. Knowing He is Holy and pure. Knowing you believe and He will come through every time. Knowing we can rejoice all of the time for He is our Divine. Knowing our hope never fades out for we know He only has good for us.

Victorious

Knowing we are the head and not the tail, above and not beneath. Knowing that no weapon formed against you will prosper. Knowing we have a covenant that cannot be broken. We are supernatural beings passing through Earth sharing the Gospel, saving lives from Hell and destruction. Knowing our children and families are saved and filled with the Holy Ghost.

> *1 Corinthians 15:57 KJV*
> *But thanks be to God, which giveth us the victory through our Lord Jesus Christ.*

Revelation

Knowing when we ask for wisdom, He gives it to us. Knowing we are His voice, His feet, His hands, His eyes, and His ears.

When we have this knowing in our hearts, our minds will always be renewed easily. For we have tapped into the very heart of God and are one with Him. Nothing can take it away, for we are established in Him.

Relationship

Christianity is not a religion; it is an intimate relationship with Jesus and our Father God. His Kingdom in us when we receive His Son Jesus into our hearts. We are eternal beings. This is salvation. We are His family. Even more than that, Jesus is our groom and the Church is His Bride. He sees us sinless, beautiful, and magnificent. We are never sinful, for He paid the price for all sins at the cross. Knowing He is waiting for the right time to come after us and we are united with Him forever. Knowing we will be at the supper table with our Jesus, dressed in white linens. Knowing we are priceless gems, without a blemish or flaw.

Hallelujah!

None Greater

Written by Deborah K. Reed
August 24, 1998

There is no silver or gold in All the lands.
That can take the place of the scars in Jesus' hands.
No rubies, diamonds, sapphires in a mound.
Can take the place of the thorns in His crown.
He is life everlasting.
He is pure as a dove that is why He died on the cross
so we could know His love.

No cattle or lands or riches untold.
Can take the place of the stripes on His back
where blessings unfold.
No fame or glory or beauty as a rose bud
can take the place of His sweat and blood.
He is life everlasting,
He is pure as a dove that is why He died on the cross
so we could know His love.

There is none greater than Jesus!

Chapter 3
Covenant Relationship

Knowing

Knowing when you have revelations of who you are in Him, there is no room for doubt. Knowing we are His vessels, He is the Captain. Knowing we can live by our spirit man, because the Holy Spirit lives within us. Knowing when we act on our faith, it will bring all promises to us. Knowing all we have to do is believe, receive, and praise; it is done. Knowing Father God gave His only Son and Jesus said, *"It is finished."*

> *2 Corinthians 4:7 NLT*
> *We now have this light shining in our hearts, but we ourselves are like fragile clay jars containing this great treasure.fn This makes it clear that our great power is from God, not from ourselves.*

Royalty

Knowing we are one with Jesus, God the Father, and the Holy Spirit. Knowing we are supernatural SUPERMEN and SUPERWOMEN of God. Knowing we are royalty, sitting beside His throne. Knowing our sins are forgiven: past, present, and future sins. Knowing we are free from condemnation. Knowing we can live a stress-free life. Knowing we see others, just as Jesus does. Knowing we are partakers of His divine nature. That we become unmovable grounded in Him and His Word. Knowing we are inseparable from Him. Knowing He has our backs covered and our fronts too. We are covered by Him always.

> *2 Peter 1:4 AMP*
> *By means of these He has bestowed on us His precious and exceedingly great promises, so that through them you may escape [by flight] from the moral decay (rottenness and corruption) that is in the world because of covetousness (lust and greed), and become sharers (partakers) of the divine nature.*

Covenant

Knowing His rich blood represents everything and protects us, our children, our assets, and our future. Knowing we have a blood covenant. Knowing everything bows to Jesus. Knowing we are free from the law of sin and death. Knowing His grace has set us free. Knowing He picked us out before we were born in our mothers' wombs.

> *Philippians 2:9-10 KJV*
> *9. Wherefore God also hath highly exalted him,*

and given him a name which is above every name:
10. That at the name of Jesus every knee should bow, of things in heaven, and things in earth, and things under the earth;

The Light

Knowing we are illuminated with His glorious light, to shine bright in this dark world. Knowing our spirits are the candle of the Lord. Knowing He has given us joy unspeakable and full of glory. Knowing He has given us a sound mind, and peace that passes all understanding. Knowing His power is the greatest in the universe. Knowing when He speaks, it happens. Knowing He gives final authority and He gets all of the glory due to Him. Knowing He is the one and only true King, Lord, and Master. Knowing He is the light and He never lies. Knowing He is pure and full of love, yet full of dynamic power.

Fellowship

Knowing you can come and dine with Him at his table. Knowing at the table is victory, prosperity, health, and everything you need. Knowing you are free to move and have your being in Him. It is the knowing that keeps our hope, our dreams, and our visions alive. Knowing we are the seed of Abraham. Knowing we are the apple of His eye. When we pray, believe, and receive it. It will be done.

Identity

Knowing as He is, so are we in this world. God sees us and loves as much as He does His own Son. Knowing Jesus has no sickness or lack, and neither do we. For we have been engrafted in Him. Knowing out of His fullness, we have received grace, spiritual blessing upon spiritual blessing, favor, and gifts. Knowing we worship Him in spirit and in truth. Knowing He believes in us constantly and reveals Himself to you.

John 1:16 NLT
From his abundance we have all received one gracious blessing after another.

Abiding

Knowing He is the vine, and we His branches. When we abide in Him we bear much fruit. Stay united in Him and His Words remain in us. If we ask anything, it shall be done. Know this honors and glorifies God. Knowing we are true followers of Him. Knowing He has planted us, that we keep on bearing much more fruit. Knowing Jesus is the way, the truth and the light. Knowing He has given us hidden treasures of the darkness. Knowing when we decree, it shall be established. Knowing hope is the anchor of our faith and resting in His Word brings our prayers to pass. Knowing He is our rock, our stronghold. Knowing we live and have our being in Him. Knowing we come from victory and end in victory.

Love

Written by Deborah K. Reed
March 2011

*Beloved, let us love one another, for love is God,
and everyone who loves is born of God.
He who does not love, does not know God.
For God is love.
I John 4:7-8*

*God gave us Jesus, our greatest gift.
Through Him we have His power to know Him intimately.
In Jesus our hearts connect to Father God.
We have a deeper relationship.
To live our lives in Him and to share with others.
This is the joy of knowing Him more.*

God's Presence

Written by Deborah K. Reed
2011

Intimacy is being filled with His love and passion.
He desires for us to come deeper in His glorious presence.
Come in, dying to self.
Draw near to Me, my glory takes over you.
The veil was torn, we can enter into the Holy of Holies.
His plan for us is to become Christlike in character.
I am your resting place.
Enter in with no cares, only to seek Me.
And allow Me to lavish my love,
Radiant presence upon you.
We are not just in Him,
But we are in His Name also...
Jes<u>us</u>!

Abiding in Intimacy

Jerusalem, Jerusalem

Written by Deborah K. Reed
April 2011

*Jerusalem, Jerusalem God's holy city, holy land.
Let's pray for and let us stand for Jerusalem, Jerusalem.
No plot in hell no scheme of man
can ever pluck it from His hand.*

*We will dwell there with the great I Am.
We will live in Jerusalem.
Jerusalem, Jerusalem God's holy city.
Holy ground.*

*Jerusalem, Jerusalem God still reigns,
I'm Jerusalem*

Midnight Hour

Written by Deborah K. Reed
November 3, 1998

*I am waiting for the midnight hour,
I am waiting for God's awesome power.
To unlock these chains that had me bound,
I kept praising, and I heard the sound.*

*It came like a mighty rush of wind,
Like the day of Pentecost, the Holy Spirit came in.
He encamped with His holy presence,
I was delivered, set free, oh the essence.*

*My spirit and soul was soaring,
overflowing, at their banks,
I fell to my knees, I worshiped and gave thanks.
He gave me wisdom, revelation, and truth to unfold,*

*Oh Jesus, Father God, Holy Spirit,
You are more precious than gold.
Each time that I am waiting for the midnight hour,
I'll be prepared again for your awesome power.*

Chapter 4
Our Inheritance

His Power

Knowing when we receive Jesus as Lord and Saviour, we are marked in Him with the seal of the Holy Spirit. This guarantees our inheritance in this life. Knowing He gives us wisdom and revelation into deep intimate knowledge of His being, His power works in us because of Jesus' resurrection and we have been given that same authority. For we sit beside Him in Heaven.

> *Ephesians 3:20 AMP*
> *Now to Him Who, by (in consequence of) the [action of His] power that is at work within us, is able to [carry out His purpose and] do superabundantly, far over and above all that we [dare] ask or think [infinitely beyond our highest prayers, desires, thoughts, hopes, or dreams]—*

His Blood

Knowing through His blood, we have redemption, forgiveness of sin. For grace has set us free. All things have been put under our feet and we have been given dominion on earth. The blessing in Jesus Christ He places in us to bring heaven on earth and all things under the Lordship of Him. Knowing we were grafted into Him and can be God-minded. His fullness within us. Knowing the depth and length of His love for us.

His Strength

We have boldness, confidence to, freedom to come to our Father anytime. Knowing He will do exceedingly and abundantly, above all we ask or think. Knowing He is glorified in me. We are out of the darkness, into His light. Knowing we are strong in Him and His might. We have the full armor of God. We stand against the principalities and powers of the wicked in the spirit realm.

> *Ephesians 6:13 NLT*
> *Therefore, put on every piece of God's armor so you will be able to resist the enemy in the time of evil. Then after the battle you will still be standing firm.*

His Love

Knowing He is real true love, His love is unconditional. Knowing His love is not self seeking or demands its own way. Knowing it is ever giving, caring about others. Knowing He is our best friend, companion, provider, physician, He is all things. Knowing we are in His family of unity and pure joy. Knowing when He corrects us it is in kindness. Knowing He is so beautiful and lovely and sees us the same way. Knowing He is the sole expression of the glory of God. The radiance of divine life.

Ephesians 2:4 KJV
But God, who is rich in mercy, for his great love wherewith he loved us,

His Goodness

Knowing our Lord reigns. Knowing He is high and lifted up, exalted above all kings. Knowing He has done marvelous things. Knowing He is good and His mercy and loving kindness are everlasting. Knowing His faithfulness and truth endures. Knowing He gives us His power to keep calm in the days of adversity. Knowing the signs of His power are revealed to us. Knowing His delightfulness and favor are upon us.

Romans 8:17-18 KJV
17. And if children, then heirs; heirs of God, and joint-heirs with Christ; if so be that we suffer with him, that we may be also glorified together.
18. For I reckon that the sufferings of this present time are not worthy to be compared with the glory which shall be revealed in us.

His Favor

Knowing He will satisfy us with long life for we trust

Him. Knowing we are planted in His home. Knowing we are living memorials. Knowing He is our Rock, He is our stronghold. Knowing He is the glory of our strength. Knowing He is a Sun and a Shield. Knowing He bestows favor, splendor and heavenly bliss. Knowing He withholds nothing from us as we walk uprightly. Knowing my only delight is our God.

Psalms 84:10-12 The Message
One day spent in your house, this beautiful place of worship, beats thousands spent on Greek island beaches. I'd rather scrub floors in the house of my God than be honored as a guest in the palace of sin.

All sunshine and sovereign is God, generous in gifts and glory. He doesn't scrimp with his traveling companions.

It's smooth sailing all the way with God-of-the-Angel-Armies.

His Light

Knowing when we sing praises to His Name, He makes His face to shine upon us. Knowing we are a green olive tree in the house of God. Knowing He causes my lamp to shine. Knowing Jesus is my chosen portion, my cup, He sustains me. Knowing He is robed and clothed with majesty. Knowing He is holy and He comes to us with light. He stretches out the heavens like a curtain.

A Psalm

Written by Deborah K. Reed
April 2006

"As I seek the face of God in the morning, I yearn for His wisdom each day.

I wait for His great joy and peace to fill me to the highest. To hear and see His calling.

His deep, endless love to overwhelm my spirit and soul. And in all His splendor I shall know His direction for my life.

For His glory to be a light in me wherever I go, whoever I see, when I give myself to Him, He covers me with strength.

Time with him alone is the greatest pleasure a person could ever want or need. His radiant beauty, His loving arms, and everlasting love. You are never alone. You are clothed with His righteousness. His ever being lives within my soul.

As we look outside of our inner being, we see God everywhere. The ground we walk on, the air we breathe. Beautiful trees and flowers with radiant colors. All unique. Skies so blue and clear waters. Majestic mountains, and seasons that change. Stars that shine at night, each have a name. Be quiet, listen to God, and you will never be the same."

Here I Am

Written by Deborah K. Reed
March 1998

*Lord, I am Yours, You have all of me,
I am Your workmanship, created in thee.
My hands will work for Your glory flow,
My feet will walk where You want them to go.
Your love will shine through my eyes for all to see,
Praise and worship will come from lips continually.
My tongue will speak Your Word with authority,
For within my heart is the greatest victory.
Father God, Jesus my Lord, Holy Spirit glorified are Thee,
I am so blessed and grateful that You dwell inside of me.*

Love of Jesus

Written by Deborah K. Reed
February 28, 2004

Fill my cup, oh Lord each and every day,
Give me compassion, have Your way.
Love is not selfish or demands its own way,
It is ever giving, to those who have gone astray.
Love is kind and patient,
It endures to the end.
Love is forgiving others,
Including the sinful and your brothers.
Love is pure and true,
Jesus' love is for you.

Jesus

Written by Deborah K. Reed
March 1994

"What passion is greater than what Christ did on cavalry?
For with His bloodshed, He gave man the choice to be free.
"No poverty, disease or lack is in Me,
nor in you when you receive Me.
I paid the price for all infirmities.
There is no greater love than I can give
and all of the blessings that come with it
as long as you may live.
No fear or turmoil shall rule in you.
With My peace and strength, all things you can do."

Oh Daddy God

Written by Deborah K. Reed
April 2010

Oh, Daddy God, I come to Thee,
As a little child upon Your knee.
Your arms around me, holding me tight,
Assuring me everything is alright.
As I walk through the streets of this land,
Doing Your work, You're holding my hand.
Your love and wisdom, all of Your might,
People will hear and receive their sight.
I thank you God, for all You have done,
For saving my soul, for giving Your Son.
There is none greater in the world than Thee,
Or a little child upon Your knee.

Survival of The Fetus

Written by Deborah K. Reed
April 2014

*Jesus saved me in my mother's womb,
Satan tried to kill me, but God gave him no room.
As a little child, I was full of joy,
I didn't even get upset when I didn't get a toy.
My friends and family said I was a lot of fun,
No one in the neighborhood could beat me when we'd run.
I always had a great, big smile upon my face,
I enjoyed being a tom girl, instead of all of the lace.
As I grew up, over the years,
Jesus took away my fears and washed away my tears.
He forgave me of all my wrong,
And put in my heart the most beautiful song.
I know He has a plan for me, and I will win my race,
That's why I am so grateful for His amazing grace.*

Abiding in Intimacy

All About Him

Written by Deborah K. Reed
January 30, 2002

*Don't think about what you need,
Possessions, self success or anything.
Just keep your eyes on Jesus alone,
Praise and worship, go to His throne.
Seek after Him and do His Word,
You will be free, like a flying bird.
Walk in His love and help mankind,
His peace and joy, you shall truly find.
The One person you need to please,
Is God Almighty in the heavenlies.
He made this world and all of us,
So give yourself to Him and trust.
We've all been given a destiny,
To love people and see them set free.
From fear or strife, hate, or hell,
Alcohol, drugs, worry, or fail.
So do your part and we all become one,
And give all of the glory to Jesus, God's Son.
He gave it all upon that tree,
And all His love is for you and me.*

Alone

Written by Deborah K. Reed
October 18, 1986

*When I feel all alone,
Trying to do things on my own.
I call on Jeremiah 33:3; God's telephone,
and go to His throne.
I fellowship, we have our talk,
He guides me in the way I should walk.*

*He takes my hand, He takes my heart,
He gives me His strength to do my part.
Everyday I know there is someone I can bless,
With joy, love, peace, or happiness.
I asked to be a guiding light,
A warrior for Him to win the fight.*

*No looking back, keep pressing on,
Casting down religions and traditions of men.
What God loves most of all,
Is when I go out and win a soul.*

Forgiveness

Written by Deborah K. Reed
1994

Forgiving is forgetting,
Remembering no more.

Don't keep those memories in your mind,
It opens Satan's door.

Put God's thoughts in their place,
Pure, honest and kind.

You will have love, joy
And a peaceful mind.

Yesterday is Gone

Written by Deborah K. Reed
1995

Yesterday is gone,
I will live for today.
Yesterday's gone,
Lord show me the way.

Lift me up with your power,
Fill me with your love.
So I can give unto others,
Receiving great things from above.

Eyes on Jesus

Written by Deborah K. Reed
1994

Keep your eyes on Jesus,
Keep your eyes on the Lord,
Confess the Word from your mouth,
It's like a mighty sword.
Satan's tactics are defeated,
He cannot do a thing,
Let's praise God, dance and sing.
Hallelujah,
HALLELUJAH!
Let's dance and sing!

Faith

Written by Deborah K. Reed
1991

I walk by faith,
Not by sight.
I walk in the power of God's might.
He sent His Son to lead us right,
To be victorious, to win the fight.

I read His Word,
I speak it out.
I get excited and I shout.
There is no fear, there is no doubt,
God is in, Satan is out.

Hallejuah, praise the Lord,
Glory to His Name.

Abiding in Intimacy

Holy Ghost

Written by Deborah K. Reed
1992

*Holy Ghost, Holy Ghost,
There is no one like the Holy Ghost.*

*Holy Ghost, Holy Ghost,
You know that He's the most,*

*Holy Ghost, Holy Ghost,
Without Him, You will roast.*

*Holy Ghost, Holy Ghost,
Let's give Him a toast!*

Favor

Written by Deborah K. Reed
2001

Favor in the restaurants, favor in stores,
favor walking in and out of all doors.

Favor with my family, favor at work,
favor with my friends and even the jerks.

Hallelujah! I have God's favor!

Best Friend

Written by Deborah K. Reed
1992

Jesus You are my best friend,
Jesus You are my Lord.
Jesus You are, Jesus You are,
Jesus You are my King.

Jesus You are my best friend,
Jesus You are my provider,
Jesus You are, Jesus You are,
Jesus You are my God.

Jesus You are my best friend,
Jesus You are my healer,
Jesus You are, Jesus You are,
Jesus You are my Lord.

Children

Written by Deborah K. Reed
1992

*Jesus loves the children,
They are precious in His sight.*

*Jesus loves the children,
With all His power and might.*

*Big or tall, little or small,
Jesus adores, He loves them all.*

Prosperity

Written by Deborah K. Reed
1992

My bills are paid, I'm out of debt,
I am prosperous.
When you believe, then receive,
For Jesus did it on the cross.
So read God's Word and do it everyday,
He will bless your soul and spirit,
And every other way.

Birthday

Written by Deborah K. Reed
1991

Happy birthday to Jesus my Saviour,
Happy birthday to Jesus my Lord,
Happy birthday to Jesus,
My Master, my King,
Happy birthday, You're my everything.

Behind

Written by Deborah K. Reed
1991

*Get behind me Satan,
In the Name of the Lord,
Jesus has set me free.
Get behind me Satan,
In the Name of the Lord,
You have no authority.*

*Jesus has set me free,
Hallejuah!*

*Jesus has set me free,
Jesus has set me free,
Hallejuah!*

Glory to His Name!

Healed

Written by Deborah K. Reed
1991

*I am healed by the stripes of Jesus,
There is healing in Jesus' Name.
I am healed by the stripes of Jesus,
I will never be the same.*

*I am healed by the stripes of Jesus,
He paid the price you see.
I am healed by the stripes of Jesus,
He died for you and me.*

Abiding in Intimacy

A Mother's Cry
Written by Deborah K. Reed
2007

Oh Lord, I know You hear a mother's cry,
I know You love my kids, and so do I.
You give me strength to nurture them,
For You are their Dad, Oh, Elohim.
You give them mercy,
You show them grace.
As long as I seek your face.
Give me wisdom in what to say,
Teach me the steps along the way.
You watch their steps from up above,
You love us all with your great love.
They will love You for You love them,
You are our God, oh, Elohim.
I have your Word, You never lie,
I know You hear a Mother's cry.

Arise, Oh Church

Written by Deborah K. Reed
March 2011

Arise oh Church,
Arise in Zion.
For I am Judah,
The mighty lion.
Seek Me and you will find Me.
Arise and take your stand,
I will pour my Spirit upon the land.
No looking to the left or to the right,
Keep going straight into the light.

Resting

Written by Deborah K. Reed
2011

We enter into God's rest by faith. Knowing is believing His finished work. His blessings are ours already. It is through Jesus we have this rest.

Jesus made the way to receive my Father's help in any situation. Knowing Jesus is our high priest forever. Knowing He lives to intercede for us. He sacrificed all sins from the past to the future.

Resting is the knowing.

Expecting His goodness to come to us. Jesus rested in God, we rest in God, because Jesus made the way for us to reconnect with our Father.

One God

Written by Deborah K. Reed
1998

There is only One God Who can truly free us.
The world says this, the world says that.
God knows your heart, He knows where you're at.
He sent His Son to die for our sins.

Come out of yourself and enter in Him.
His love never fails, His peace will not part.
Praise Him with your lips, worship with your heart.
Meditate in His Word day and night.

Walk by faith, and not by sight.
Learn to know Him and you will win.
You will be fulfilled unto the end.
For there is only One God Who can truly free us.

Awakening

Written by Deborah K. Reed
February 2015

God told His people if they would humble themselves and pray and seek His face. Turn from their wicked ways, that He would heal their land.

A great move of God's glory must take place, but we must do as God says. We must be humble, stay in purity and prayer. This manifests His love among us. We are standing and believing for Him to visit us in a tremendous outpouring. United together in spirit with our first love.

The fervent prayer of a righteous man availeth much.

We must stay in expectation of His visitation upon the Earth. We must allow Him to be in full reign in church meetings and homes.

Religion, legalism, culture style must go. *It is not by power or might but by my Spirit says the Lord.*

When we let go and die to ourselves, desiring the depth of our God. Allowing Him to have control, healings, deliverances, miracles occur. We must come together in unity of His Spirit. Soaking in His glorious presence. We are filled with such joy and love and peace.

Knowing we can rejoice always. We are changed from glory to glory. We are victors, heirs, truly blessed.

Amen.

Prophecy

Written by Deborah K. Reed
June 15, 2013

Sow His seed upon His ground, the rock of our salvation. When you sow my Word, it brings my Kingdom of living in your life. Nothing can stop it for I am the creator, the Almighty God. When you have faith in Me and my Word and start praising Me. Knowing I will perform it, it will happen. You have the anointing, for I the anointed One lives in you. Sow to Jesus all that He is from a pure heart established in Him, you have the Keys to my Kingdom, for you belong to Me. You are my family.

No more destruction, no more delays. May blessings come your way. From afar, near towns, flowing all around. Liquid love pouring down. Mercies great, Mercies small. Meeting the needs of all. Illuminating light shining down from above. My presence will rest like a dove. Invasion of power, a spring of my flower will rise upon this Earth and bring new birth. To the young, to the old, as the prophet has told. It is time for the awakening, a rise of dead bones. Miracles will happen ever so fast, rejoice, and your prayers will suddenly come to pass. A bride who is so in love with Me will be glorified, setting this world on fire, setting men free. A love so great, grace so vast, a relationship that never dies, only lasts. It is all by my Spirit, all by my love. Keep your faith in Me, keep looking above. My glory will glisten from mountains to the seas. Upon all valleys, grass and trees. Covering the Earth, there will be many cries. Holy Ghost laughter will then arise.

Prophecies

Written by Deborah K. Reed
August 7, 2012

It is the worst of times for the world's systems and ways.

This is the best of time for my Kingdom and my way.

Those who are in Jesus Christ, you are living in the greatest days known to man.

As the world gets darker, I become brighter. And those who stay in my presence, will glow and shine with my light and spirit.

Your spirits are a flame of fire. Our lamps should always be filled with oil and keep burning with his anointing and power.

For the greatest and most awesome possession is Him and Him alone, Jesus. As He gets brighter, His glory will shine all over the world, His saints shining right along with Him.

Many changes will occur in a short time. Suddenly earthquakes will appear in the Earth, then an earthquake in the Spirit. Volcanoes will erupt, then a volcano of my power will erupt. Floods will occur, then floods of my power in love will occur, bringing many to receive Me. An exchange of disaster for awakening to Me, love and peace as never known before.

Wars will rage, yet I will reign in and among my people. For they will not fear. For my strength is mighty among them.

Stay close to Me, always hear my voice and know when the wind blows and the seas roars and the trees are talking. Always be aware of things taken place in the Spirit. We will accomplish what He has planned together.

Remember to pray without ceasing, giving thanks, praise, worship in my Holy Temple. Stay rooted and grounded in Me and my Word. Not moving to the left or the right. Be bold, rise up, and declare my works. *"Stand for me,"* says the Lord God Almighty, *"for I am with thee always."*

Stay filled with my love, peace, compassion, and mercy. And walk in it and share it out everywhere you go. Stay in my presence. Walk in it, move in it, and rejoice in it.

For when all is finished, the trumpet sounds, the Eastern sky will split. All will see Me in my glory and I will take my people home with Me in just a twinkle of an eye. Rejoice for the hour is coming, so keep your eyes, ears, and heart stedfast and soon you will be with me forever. Amen.

Conclusion

Everyone born has a spirit and a soul in a live flesh body. The body is flesh, the soul is intellect and emotions, and the spirit is the real man. I know God is real and Jesus is His Son, the Messiah, Who died for man's sins. He gave man a choice to choose life or death. To live by the world's knowledge or to receive Jesus in their hearts. To follow God's way, not our own.

I know He lives in me, for I have joy and peace and love that this world could never give me. He walks with me all of the time, He never leaves me. I have felt His glorious hand upon me and kept me healed of infirmities. He has helped me through distresses that come in my life. He knows everything and will answer when you call upon Him.

Jesus willingly obeyed Father God and was persecuted, and beaten beyond recognition, just so people could be free from evil.

Everyone wants to be loved in this world, but the real, true love is knowing Jesus and our Father God. When a person receives Jesus and becomes born again, they want no hate, strife, or fear. He will only want peace. We are forgiven of our sins and have a whole new life to live. It's a relationship with the Almighty. Who instructs, guides, warns, and loves us with all of His heart. Knowing we rest in Him, for He finished it all. How glorious is this?

A Soul Winner's Heart

Do you desire true love, joy, peace, direction, success, relationships, healing, and family restoration?

John 3:16
"For God so loved the world, that he gave his only begotten son. That, whosoever believes in him shall not perish, but have eternal life."

Romans 10:9-10
"That if you confess with your mouth, Jesus is Lord, and believe in your heart that God raised him from the dead, you will be saved.
For with the heart, a person believes, resulting in righteousness, and with the mouth he confesses, resulting in salvation."

Prayer for Salvation

"Dear Heavenly Father,

I pray in the Name of Jesus.
I know You lived a sinless life and died on the cross as my substitute taking the full punishment for my sins. I believe You raised to life 3 days later winning complete victory for me over sin, sickness, poverty and death.
I come to You now based on Your Word in the Book of John which says,

John 6:37
He that cometh to me, shall not be cast out.

I believe God raised Jesus Christ from the dead and He is now seated in power at the righthand of The Father.

Romans 10:13
Whosoever shall call upon the name of the Lord shall be saved.

Jesus because You lived, died and now live forever, I

confess You as Lord. I give myself to You, take me and make me what You want me to be. I acknowledge Your Lordship in all things.

Romans 10:9-10
If you acknowledge and confess with your lips that Jesus is Lord and in your heart believe that God raised him from the dead, you will be saved.

JESUS YOU ARE LORD OF MY LIFE!

Thank You for saving me, I am Your child. Use me to do Your will; I will confess You before men as Lord of my life. Praise You Jesus! Amen!"

Reference Scriptures

Chosen Generation
Ephesians 1:1-23, 2:1-10

Free From the Law
Romans 8:1-3, 14-17
I Peter 1:1-4
Revelations 21:7

God Gave His Son
I John 3:16

Healing
Isaiah 53:1-5
I Peter 2:24

Heirs to His Kingdom
Hebrews 1:2
Galatians 2:20, 3:13, 4:6-7

Love
I Corinthians 13:4-8

Redemption
John 3:16, 6:37
Romans 10:9-13
Colossians 2:1-10, 3:1-17

Notes:

Deborah is available for Field Ministry,
Speaking Engagements and...
"Fire Meetings"

Deborah currently resides in Tulsa, Oklahoma.
She can be contacted at:
debbykaye777@yahoo.com

Check out these other Great Books from BOLD TRUTH PUBLISHING

by Adrienne Gottlieb
- **ISRAEL'S LEGITIMACY**
Why We Should Protect Israel At All Cost

- **The Replacement Theology LIE**
The Book Jews wished every Christian would read

-----

by Daryl Holloman
- **Seemed Good to The Holy Ghost**
Inspired Teachings by Brother Daryl
PLUS - Prophecies spoken in Pardo, Cebu, Philippines

- **The Adventures of Hezekiah Hare & Ernie Byrd**
A Children's Bible Adventure

- **Further Adventures**
More Good News as Hezekiah & Ernie follow Jesus.

-----

by Steve Young
- **SIX FEET DEEP**
Burying Your Past with Forgiveness

-----

by Paul Howard
- **THE FAITH WALK**
Keys to walking in VICTORY!

------

by Joe Waggnor
- **Bless THE KING**
Praise Poems for My Lord and Saviour

by Jerry W. Hollenbeck
• The KINGDOM of GOD
An Agrarian Society
Featuring The Kingdom Realities, Bible Study Course, Research and Development Classes

---

by Martha (Marti) McNabb
• THE POWER of GOD
The Power of God will help us to live in The Kingdom of God while we are here on earth.

---

by Ed Marr
• C. H. P.
Coffee Has Priority
The Memoirs of a California Highway Patrol - Badge 9045

---

by Mary Ann England
• Women in Ministry
From her Teachings at the FCF Bible School - Tulsa, Oklahoma (Foreword by Pat Harrison)

---

by James Jonsten
• WHO is GOD to YOU?
The path to know the most misunderstood name in the universe.

---

by Aaron Jones
• In the SECRET PLACE of THE MOST HIGH
God's Word for Supernatural Healing, Deliverance and Protection

• SOUND from HEAVEN
Praying in Tongues for a Victorious Life

See more Books and all of our products at www.BoldTruthPublishing.com

You will be REIGNITED, ENCOURAGED and BUILT-UP IN YOUR FAITH as Missionary Pastor & Author Daryl P Holloman shares his inspired MASTERWORK

"Daryl has a calling to empower the Body of Christ with powerful teaching and preaching of God's Word."
--David Barber
Missionary / Evangelist

"Like pages from the Book of Acts, being friends with Daryl Holloman is an adventure. He is a true Christ-like example of Love, Joy, Faith and Patience."
--Aaron Jones
Revivalist and Author

"I just love Jesus, Brother. That's all. I just love Jesus!"
-- Daryl P Holloman
Missionary pastor and Author

6"x9" over 300 pages
ISBN-13: 978-0-9904376-1-1

Available now at select Bookstores and www.BoldTruthPublishing.com

www.ingramcontent.com/pod-product-compliance
Lightning Source LLC
Chambersburg PA
CBHW061505040426
42450CB00008B/1493